Getting Out Of My Own Way

Paul Doran

Published by Paul Doran
First printing: 2014.
ISBN-13: 978-1500368043
ISBN-10: 1500368040

British Cataloguing Publication Data
A catalogue record of this book is available from The British Library.

Also available on Kindle from Amazon

Here's the Deal

I don't need to make a penny from this book. The central idea, 'Getting out of my own way', has already made me wealthy in lots of ways. Any profits from this book will go to my chosen charity. What I really care about is leaving behind a written record for my daughters, Cara and Anya. I also care that as many people as possible get access to my story. Even at the risk of revealing my own personal challenges to the world.

It's my choice to talk about myself. How I've overcome my own challenges. I'm unique. What worked for me might not work for you. So come with an open mind. Nobody has all the answers. We are all trying to figure this stuff out.

I'm going to share with you the life challenges I've faced. Sometimes it might make uncomfortable reading. Life's like that. I'll also share how I've overcome those challenges. Books I read. People I met. What worked. What didn't work.

It took over forty years for me to realise that I'd spent most of my life in my own way. My wish is that my daughters take the information and realise that they are perfect just as they are, but that sometimes they may inadvertently get in their own way. More importantly, they can get out of their own way.

You don't need to do anything in life to feel good about yourself. Nothing you achieve in the world will ever bring you lasting happiness. There is no path to happiness, because happiness is the path. You just choose to be happy.

That said, what the hell does 'choosing to be happy' actually mean? This is my answer to that question. I get out of my own way.

Contents

Introduction 7

Foundation 10

Part One: What do I believe is true about the world?............. 15

Part Two: Values 31

Part Three: What is life all about? 55

What's Next?.. 67

Appendix 1: Reading List 69

Appendix 2: Laminate.. 70

About the Author... 71

Introduction

I can remember lying on my bed, curled up in a ball. I spent a lot of time on that bed as I grew up. I was crying my eyes out. I kept repeating in my head: "Why?" Over and over. Every now and then I'd say it out loud between sobs. "Why?"

It was the question I was asking myself. The question I was asking the universe. 'Why?' I was 40 years old before I figured it out.

I'd fight. Steal. Lie. Spit. Destroy everything. My parents were at their wits' end with me. My mum refused to have some Ritalin-like drug prescribed to calm me down. They'd probably call it ADHD nowadays, but back then a few people called it 'Hyperactivity'. Most people called it being a 'naughty little bastard'.

I spent the majority of my time in the headmaster's office for fighting. One teacher told my mum: "If looks could kill then I'd be dead by now." This pretty much sums up my schooling experience. I left one primary school for continually running out of the school gates. I was about eight years old at the time.

Yet still I would ask myself why I was doing all these things. I hated myself for doing so many destructive things. I hated myself for destroying friendships because I failed to control my words and actions. I felt utterly confused. It was like having a split personality. Jekyll and Hyde.

One minute I could be the sweetest kid alive. A really naturally loving kid. No harm to anybody. I'd do anything for others. Give you my last sweet. Then the slightest little thing would set me off and I'd scare the shit out of people I was so aggressive.

Even adults became very wary around me.

Then I'd be alone. In my bedroom. Or sitting in a park somewhere. Often I'd take myself away from people. It was safer for me, and it was safer for them.

As I got older I self medicated by obsessing over everything. In my early teens it was swimming. As I got into my late teens it was bodybuilding. In recent years it was business and money.

February 2014. Yes, it took that long for somebody on a planet of seven billion people to explain what the fuck was going on in my head. I'd travelled to Yorkshire to meet, along with others, a guy who had previously worked with psychopaths in secure prisons. Apt, really. Steve Peters.

Steve started by showing us a video of Ronnie O'Sullivan throwing a fit whilst he played an important shot against Stephen Hendry in a big snooker championship. He asked us all what we thought had happened. I suppose everybody fell into the trap of repeating exactly what we had seen. Steve became slightly disgruntled by the answers, or maybe it was just for show.

Either way, he impressed upon us all that Ronnie hadn't thrown a fit at the table. He was being hijacked and had little or no control over his actions. More importantly, Steve had written a book about how a person could stop being hijacked. This made the hairs on the back of my neck stand on end. I'd felt hijacked my entire life. Like I was being inhabited by some mischievous chimp.

I was very emotional for the remainder of the weekend. Very emotional. There was a quiz for attendees later that night in the hotel bar. I didn't want to go. I was questioning why I felt so anxious about it. It took all my energy to go down to the bar that night.

When I returned to my room I pretty much broke down crying. Only this time it was pure relief. I'd spent forty years trying to understand what was going on in my head and this guy explained it all in no time.

By the time Sunday came around, I was emotionally exhausted. But it genuinely felt like the first day of a new life. I've never looked back. Life has got better and better since that day.

Steve encouraged me to ask three questions. What do I believe is true about the world around me? What do I value? How do I believe I should live my life? In hindsight, it was a blueprint for who I am.

This book is a written record of the blueprint that I created for myself. I've used events from my life to show how answering these questions has helped me. Struggles, challenges and upheaval. More importantly, it's therapy. Once I'm done writing this book I'm never looking back again at these events. I've written this for my two daughters, Cara and Anya. It may also help others.

Foundation

Before I answer those three questions, I want to share how I created a foundation for a practice that I call 'getting out of my own way'. To build anything that lasts it has to be built on a solid foundation.

The world can seem so fucked up sometimes. Last year I spoke to a customer late one Friday night. I called back on the Monday and his work colleague told me he'd jumped off a bridge over the weekend. I've had tough times in my life but I've never remotely considered this as an option.

I'm always hesitant writing about this kind of thing. I look around at all the successful and beautiful people in the world that just seem to glide around. Maybe what I'm about to write only applies to me. I've no idea!

I've had times in my life where I've felt like I had literally no money, no friends, no prospects, no family, poor health, overweight, addictions etc. At times like these it always seems like people can't wait to kick you while you're down. It's not true, but it has felt like that at times.

So here are the eight ways that I create a solid foundation to get out of my own way. Secretly I'm hoping they work for you, too.

1. You're being hijacked. Constantly. Your brain has many different parts that work together. One part of the brain tends to be much stronger in most people. It's the part that I like to call the 'Bubble Machine'. Steve Peters called it the 'chimp'.

It pumps out random emotional thoughts based on what is happening around you. It tells you that somebody hates you when they fail to smile back at you. It tells you to eat a packet of biscuits even though you just had your tea. It tells you that your wife is fooling around with her work colleague just because she mentioned a joke he told her.

The only problem is that these thoughts are beyond your control. You're being hijacked.

Learn to watch out for these thoughts. Write them down, but don't act on them. Later, after you've forgotten about them, take out the piece of paper and analyse if any of the points had any merit. Logically. Rationally. Without emotion. Most of my thoughts are limiting, random, and have no basis in facts.

2. Pick who is in your crew. Once you realise that your brain is capable of hijacking you, it will allow you to work out who is lifting you up, and who is bringing you down. Hang with people who lift you up, and swerve people who bring you down. Don't worry if you end up with only one person/animal on that list. Start small and work your way out into the world. Try to lift people up and you will attract others of a similar mind.

3. No shit. No alcohol. It's a depressant. No junk food. It will stop you from taking a shit. Not good. Eat whole foods. No recreational drugs. Cut out all toxins in your environment. Get some fresh air every day. Take a 15-20 minute walk. The return on investment is 64,000% from taking a 15 minute walk. Don't set goals. Just be kind to yourself.

4. Sleep. Sleep as much as you can. Try to get 8-9 hours of uninterrupted sleep. It's hard if you have kids. The sleep cycle is 25 hours long and the whole body goes through a total renewal process. Google 'sleep hygiene'. Stay away from 'screens' after your tea. Don't eat anything after 6pm. Prepare for bedtime by following advice given by experts in the sleep hygiene field. Insomnia is a very solvable problem

5. Gratitude. Write down everything you're grateful for right now. There is always something to be grateful for. You will have to sweat the gratitude muscle initially to think of things you are grateful for. Being grateful pushes the emphasis away from us and onto others. It's awesome.

6. Exercise idea muscle. Write down ten ideas. Don't worry about them being any good as you're going to throw them away anyhow. Get so good at coming up with ideas that if you were stuck under a rock in a canyon your idea muscle would get you out of the shit. Sweat it.

7. Slow down. All good things come when your mind is still. Find ways to get the snow globe of your mind to settle. I have used meditation since a very early age to get this effect but I've also found steam baths, music, running and sex to be useful. Experiment and find your own methods. We are all unique.

8. Write. Write a few sentences each night after you've finished your day. I put my kids to bed, take half an hour to play on my games console: 'Splinter Cell', as I write this. Then I have a diary/pen handy to write down significant emotional issues that have cropped up during the day. It's good to get it all out of your head. Often I review my entries and look for any patterns. This was how I spotted that even a few drinks at the weekend significantly impaired my moods for the rest of the week. It's also how I established what rogue codes were operating in my subconscious.

I wish I could keep up all these things long term. I'd be amazing. I struggle to keep it up once my life sorts itself out but it always gets me off the floor. It has never failed me. I've

12

achieved some amazing things that nobody ever thought I'd do and these are the methods that did it for me. Any worldly success I've ever had has come from using these tactics to create a foundation for a life centred around 'getting out of my own way'.

Success is a by-product of being healthy, showing gratitude, being an energy giver, inspiring others, being a good giver, sleeping, eating well, looking after your crew and calming your mind.

Once I'd laid the foundation I was able to focus on creating a blueprint for how I wanted to live my life. Remember those three questions? No? Well, here they are again:

1. What do I believe is true about the world?

2. What do I value?

3. What do I think life is all about?

Before I answer them there is something I need to explain.

Steve Peters explained to me how the mind consists of three working parts: the human, chimp and computer. The chimp is just an emotional thinking machine. It is five times faster than the human, so the human (you) is on a hiding to nothing. The saving grace is that the human can input into the computer, and the chimp doesn't think for itself. Whatever goes into the computer the chimp will accept as a command.

It took a while for me to answer the three questions but the real work started once I'd written it all down. I found pictures that would represent each answer. I put them all on one piece of A4, laminated it, and put copies everywhere I thought I'd see them. I rehearsed the answers every single day, four to five times a day, for a couple of months. Eventually I imprinted the answers that follow onto my internal hard drive. I've never looked back.

It made an incredible difference to my life. I'm less anxious, happier, confident, calmer, more forgiving of others, and good fun. For the first time in my life I'm consistently staying out of my own way. I realised that all the good things in my life were a direct result of practising what I'm writing about here. It's just that previously it had all happened by chance. Now I had powerful methods - that worked for me - that were repeatable.

So whenever you see me refer to my 'laminate' you now know that it's my blueprint for who I am!

Part One:
What do I believe is true about the world?

1. Life isn't fair

In the 1983 film 'Turkey Shoot', 'social deviants' are sent to prison camps for re-education and behaviour modification. After suffering brutal treatment at the hands of Camp Master and his chief enforcer, the prisoners accept a deadly deal. They will be human prey in a 'turkey shoot'. If they can evade the heavily armed guests in the surrounding jungle until sundown, the prisoners will be set free.

This sums up my teenage years growing up in Bootle during the 1980s. Only I'd have to repeat the game every night.

Unlike a lot of kids in my neighbourhood at the time, I was into computers. I had like-minded friends in different areas. It sounds odd telling this story now. Having to move within a three mile radius of our house at night led to crossing many different gang territories. The kids in these areas knew who belonged on 'their' streets and who didn't.

I'd mentally rehearse my routes every night before I set off. I'd work out alternative routes in the event that certain routes were blocked. I'd use the alleyways ('enchries') that ran between the long streets of terraced houses.

One night I turned onto Peel Road having come through a series of 'enchries' to find a gang on the corner of Scott Street. I could feel my heart beating faster. I was late getting home. Ultimately, I was more afraid of my dad than these loons. I decided to try and run past them.

"There's Doran!" shouted the ring leader. I legged it as fast as

15

I could without looking back. Being chased by a pack of kids carrying Samurai swords, bats with nails in and a devil dog is no fun.

Just as I thought I'd outrun them an offshoot of the 'Rimrose Road' gang came out of Si's Newsagents and collared me. Dragged whimpering back to the main gang, I begged them to let me go. They took me down one of the 'enchries' off Shelley Street and battered me. Let their devil dog bite me. Put a lit cigarette into the corner of my eye. Pissed on my legs as one of them sat across my chest. 'Twatted' me in the face, over and over.

The next night I set off to meet some friends over the 'raller' (railway lines) in Litherland. Life wasn't fair!

I learnt lots of things from these nightly manoeuvrings but ultimately I didn't realise the biggest lesson until I looked back all these years later.

"Life isn't fair." It's the first of my truths of life. Not only do I believe that this is one of the ways the world works, but I can point to many examples to prove that it is the case. I know it to be true. No matter how much I wish it not to be the case.

Before I recognised what was happening within my own head I held the opposite point of view. I believed that life was fair. Life should be fair. No wonder I got upset so easily. Often.

It's funny. I studied Buddhism for ten years. It never truly sank in that so many people are trying to tell us essentially the same thing. Here is what the Buddha had to say on the matter:

"You should know suffering."

As the 'turkey shoot' progressed, the tables were turned, and the prisoners became the hunters, culminating in a free-for-all slaughter. Most of the kids who chased me ended up as addicts, dead or incarcerated.

Life isn't fair. Deal with it.

2. Not everybody will like you

When I was very young I was diagnosed with 'Hyperactivity'. At the time, the only help that was available was to be given Ritalin or some other zombie drug. My mum refused. I'm so glad that she did. I'm sure everybody has their own views on the use of drugs for mental health issues. We are all unique.

One of the symptoms I had as a child is that I'd become aggressive and at times violent towards those around me. Initially that didn't matter. Bash the kid next to me just because I couldn't control my impulses. So what?!

However, it wasn't long before the teachers took note and my mum was hauled before the headmaster. This happened a lot. It didn't take long until most of the other kids would shun me. Then I was effectively pushed out of one primary school and into the next one.

As I got a bit older it started to dawn on me that my behaviour had consequences. Few friends. It also led to issues between my own family and me. It wasn't a situation that I enjoyed. I used to cry in my room. "Why am I doing this?" I'd say out loud to myself. This often led to self-loathing.

As I got into my teens I had a very bad self image issue. I'd been told often enough how 'bad' I was. So I'd hang around with kids that had been given a similar label. A toxic cocktail. Often I'd just avoid everybody. Bizarrely, I'd get plenty of attention from girls, and I'd get invited to go places with other teens. I'd never go.

By the time that I was late teens I'd developed a complex where I thought everybody hated me. So I'd take some pretty extreme measures to avoid everybody. Sitting on the cliffs at the beach. Alone. Going off on bike rides all day. Alone. That kind of explains why I've always read so many books. There isn't much else to do when you spend so much time alone.

By the time I was ready to go to college I'd realised that I had to do something about this issue. I'd started to read books about psychology. I recognised a lot of the issues that I was reading about in the books. These self help books helped me to practise methods for getting along with people better. It worked. However, it came with a sting in the tail.

After being such a social misfit for so long, I soon found these self help methods working and I'd think that everybody should like me. Maybe I couldn't accept that my new Harry Potter skills couldn't work on everybody. It was almost as though if everybody didn't like me then I was a failure. My self-worth had become tied to the opinion of others.

Clearly this is ridiculous. I think we would all agree that it's impossible to be liked by everybody. However, I started to understand how fast and strong my internal hard drive (subconscious mind) actually is. Often we are simply not aware of what is stored inside our mental computers and how it affects our lives. I had a program running that stated:

IF (somebody) 'like' NOT (you) THEN 'do whatever it takes' TO (win) them OVER. IF 'not' THEN LOOP.

OK. OK. OK. It's a poor attempt to write code for a human

computer. But hopefully you get the general idea. I'd cause myself untold pain in trying to execute a line of code in my head that simply could never execute. Whilst this line of code was trying to execute I was incapable of doing anything else.

I was preoccupied with trying to get everybody to like me.

So one of the first truths of life that I developed for myself was that 'Not everybody will like me'. I know that this is true because I've developed this truth through direct experience of life. I'm sure lots of people have. I'd be keen to hear from anybody who didn't believe it was a truth of life.

On the first few days of rehearsing my **'laminate'** (remember-that important document?) I found it very clumsy, and it didn't really seem to work. I'd still get frustrated with people who didn't seem to get me, or people who criticised my ideas and work. However, after a few weeks I started to notice something really odd. Exciting.

I was helping out a guy on a forum with an issue he was having, and some 'anonymous' character (they are always anonymous – have you noticed?) jumped into the conversation and started to assassinate my advice. I could feel my hackles rising, which normally would have cycled through rumination, counter attack, followed by self-loathing. Only this time it didn't happen.

So what did happen?! The picture I'd chosen to remind me that not everybody will like me came into my mind and I calmed down instantly. I wasn't really thinking about it. It just came to mind. Magic. I was so excited that I ran off to tell my wife. She must have thought I was 'barking', given I was so excited.

You see, I was excited that I was no longer bothered about everybody liking me. But more than that, it was the confirmation that I finally had a repeatable method to tackle any mental problem I had.

And, just like that, I felt my depression lift. I had no idea that I was depressed. Once it lifted, I knew. Slowly my energy levels have started to come back. I'm not where I want to be but I feel like I'm pointing in the right direction now. I also feel it's a duty to help, where I'm able, to point others in the right direction. Hence this book.

I liken this process to learning to drive a car. At first it feels impossible. There are too many things to think about. But then, slowly, some of the tasks just automate and we are unaware of gear changes and mirror checks. Before long we can eat sandwiches and fiddle with iPhones whilst we drive (not recommended but I think it makes the point well).

I don't even see the images on my laminated document any more. I just feel much much calmer when people appear to not like me or agree with me. My explanation is that the line of code in my computer is now hard wired and executes so fast I'm no longer aware of the process.

I know not everybody will like me. However, I do believe that I increase the probability that you might ... simply by my acceptance of this truth of life.

Not everybody will like me – I deal with it.

3. Nothing lasts forever

In the October of 2008 I became obsessed with the machinations of banking, economics and finance. I do really mean obsessed. The sub-prime crisis had brought the world to the brink, although I don't think people really appreciated how close we had come.

I'd spend 8-10 hours per day reading about the history of money and how fiat currency systems work. I'd spend hours delving into how CDOs had infected the whole system. When TARP failed its first vote, I had a telephone conversation with my brother, who is a bond manager in the city. We were both incredulous that they had failed to understand what would happen if AIG et al went under the following morning. I'd lose everything I'd worked so hard for.

At first it was scary. The more I studied the more I began to see the bigger picture. Money is simply a means of exchange for goods and services. Saving is simply deferred spending. You aren't meant to keep it. For the first time in my life I could see the futility of trying to cling onto things that aren't designed to last. Perhaps those voting TARP down had already understood this lesson. Nothing lasts forever.

I love helping my kids make sandcastles when we go on holiday in the summer time. Building out the basic structure of castles. Double stacking. Scraping out a moat to protect the imaginary inhabitants from invasion. Running up and down the beach to fetch water for the moat. Ace!

My kids aren't of the age yet that they show any signs of worrying about what happens to their creations when we head home. They look forward to building another one the next day. They enjoy the build rather than the possession. Like they instinctively know that nothing lasts forever.

It's not a throwaway society mentality. Just an acceptance of basic reality. When all other sensible options have been exhausted, I'm happy to accept that nothing lasts forever.

Recently, I'd had lots of problems with my boiler at home. It was going to cost £6K to replace, and part of my brain felt that the insurance company were trying to get out of the maintenance contract.

This may well have been accurate, but I didn't have any real evidence to support that supposition. The senior manager visited the house. I could feel my hackles rising and the bubble machine inside my head started producing random thoughts. Playing out events. Moving chess pieces within my head.

"Throw him out of the house." "Tell him to fucking fix the thing." "Lie about the nature of the problems."

Prior to getting out of my own way, I'd have followed one of these random suggestions that my bubble machine pumped out. I mistook them as commands. Later on I'd have justified my actions and then felt fucking awful. I know that I'm a nice decent person. I used to get hijacked constantly. Less and less these days.

Like a slow moving scene in a movie, I could see/hear/feel this internal dialogue going on; then it just evaporated. I resigned myself to handling the guy compassionately. I'm sure he didn't want to be here, potentially giving me bad news. I thought for a brief moment why I had become so calm.

I recalled my image of 'nothing lasts forever'. That picture of a crumbling 'Colosseum' came to mind instantly. I wasn't aware of it at the time, but it definitely explained why I had calmed down.

The boiler is over 15 years old. It will not last forever. My dog is 7 years old. He will not last forever. I've done quite nicely from the businesses I've built. The proceeds will not last forever. The financial system has been stabilised. By its very nature that situation won't last forever. Nothing lasts forever.

I'm thinking about building sandcastles with my little monsters this summer. It's going to be ace.

4. You might not wake up tomorrow

In April 2014 I flew over the Irish Sea to Derry, Northern Ireland. My friend was getting married the next day, Saturday. There wasn't a lot happening the night before, so I went for a long walk in the rain. On the way I found a half decent looking Chinese restaurant. I pigged out.

By the time I got back to the hotel it was quite late. I spotted a text message from my brother-in-law. Seemed odd, but nothing out of the ordinary. We got on very well but didn't really keep in touch outside of family events. The text asked me to give him a call back. I was too tired so decided to call him back in the morning.

See also: too lazy

I slept like a baby that night. Really deep REM. Woke up. Scratched my arse. Brushed my teeth. Took a piss. Rituals. Then my phone rang.

"The kids...the kids...the kids are fine," I heard my wife's panic-stricken voice say. Then the crying and emotion flooded down the phone. I couldn't get any sense out of her for a while. She'd been at the hospital all night with her sister.

I managed to get her to calm down long enough to explain what had happened. During the night my brother-in-law had been found in the street, with his dog sitting next to him. Motionless. Lifeless. A massive aneurysm had exploded inside his head and he was effectively dead on arrival. They hooked him up to life support to allow his family the opportunity to say some goodbyes.

I immediately remembered the text message.

It was a mad dash to get back from the world's smallest airport, Derry. No planes were due to fly out that day. My only option was to get a taxi across to Belfast and see if I could get a flight home later that day. Luckily there was a flight available. I remember feeling a huge sense of gratitude that I was going to see my kids that night.

I also remember thinking ... you might not wake up tomorrow. You just don't know.

It sounds like quite a macabre thought. Who wants to contemplate death? I think I've always known that I might die. I've given it some thought. I'd considered dying in old age. I'd also considered being told that I might have six months to live and dying in a hospice. But not once did I ever consider taking the dog for a walk and dropping down on the spot. Like an off switch being flicked.

I'd always thought that I could make amends tomorrow. Make the most of tomorrow. Give people I love extra special hugs tomorrow. I'd never considered that it's not guaranteed that tomorrow will ever come.

See also: Game changer

Through this experience, I believe that I might not wake up tomorrow. So it's one of my truths of life. I don't find it at all stressful to think this way. In fact, I find it extremely liberating. And, since I've been rehearsing this truth every day, it has impacted my life in very powerful ways.

How so?!

I can't speak for other people. But I've had a tendency throughout my life to project forward. I'll go there tomorrow. Save that money for tomorrow. Make that call tomorrow. Own up tomorrow. The problem with that way of thinking is that tomorrow never comes. I never get round to doing the important stuff I need to do. Some people literally don't ever get the chance. Tomorrow never comes for them.

Nowadays this truth of life is firmly implanted on my internal hard drive. It's given me the clarity and confidence to make really important decisions. Whenever I start getting anxious about having an awkward conversation with somebody, it really helps me follow through.

I'm a natural worrier when it comes to money. This truth helps me overcome my scarcity mentality and find a balance between spending and saving.

If I'm tired at the end of a day it helps motivate me to put a bit of extra *ooomph* into the kids' bedtime stories. A bit more effort into bringing Winnie the Pooh to life for them.

When I go to bed with the wife I'll take a bit more time to cuddle and tell her how much she means to me. Rather than just a quick peck on the check if nookie isn't on the cards.

It sits on my hard drive and acts as a prompt. Life is precious and I'm not going to take it for granted.

I might not wake up tomorrow.

In the next life I'll make that return call.

Gaz. R.I.P

5. The goal posts move

Around the age of eleven we got a dog. As far as I was concerned it was my dog. Honey was a cross between a Golden Retriever and a Labrador. I loved that dog so much. It's the first time I'd ever experienced love for anything. I was a pretty destructive kid.

I don't actually remember taking it for a walk or anything like that. But I remember just sitting for hours stroking it. I loved that it seemed so happy to see me when I got home from school.

The area we lived in was right next to Liverpool Docks. At the time they were storing huge piles of coal dust on those docks. The wind would pick up and the coal dust would land on our washing. It would come through any little openings and we'd find it on the inside of the window sills, on our beds and even in our clothes. My brother developed a shadow on his lung and, eventually, asthma. Looking back, I think the coal dust was the issue, but the doctors suggested to my parents that it was the dog. Who knows?! The dog went the very next day.

I was angry about losing Honey. It was the one thing in life that made me feel calm. The one 'person' that was happy to see me. This is how I felt at the time. I was angry at my parents for taking the dog away. I took it out on my brother. Sorry, Kev.

The goal posts move. It's a truth of life. Or at least it is for me.

Think about it! How often do we make arrangements in life

only to find that some fucker messes them up? For me, it happens all the time – and it really pisses me off. Or at least it did.

I own a hazardous waste company. If I had to give an elevator pitch to a Dragon, I'd say that we make arrangements to collect waste from one location and take it to another location. Given it's hazardous waste there is a lot more to it than that, but ultimately that is what we do.

Those arrangements are often changed by others, without warning, and often to my financial cost. Seemingly there is little I can do about it. It's the main reason that I hated it for so many years.

I'd been practising imprinting these ideas on my internal hard drive for a few weeks. Recently I set up a collection of an old redundant petrol tank. The guy doing the collection let me down a few hours before it was due. Some guff about a truck being on the wrong side of the moon. In this industry, you hardly ever hear the truth. Never mind.

I could feel/hear the bubble machine kicking in. Angry thoughts coming to the surface that would normally end in a volley of abuse being sent down the wire to the person at the other end of the phone. Almost instantly, the image of somebody moving the goal posts sprung into my head. The goal posts move.

I kept my cool with the guy. I asked him for a realistic time when he could complete the collection. Thanked him. Rang the customer and agreed a new collection date. He didn't seem that bothered. Kettle on. Job done.

I smiled. I'd not done that, in this situation, for a long long time. Perhaps ever. Had I cracked it?

I'm starting to notice positive outcomes in all areas of my life, such as:

Not getting frustrated if me and the missus plan to 'hook up' and just as we are getting into bed one of the babies wakes up.

Sometimes I make arrangements with friends and family to meet for dinner etc. They often aren't as punctual as I am. I'm very reliable if you arrange to meet me at a set time. It has often frustrated me if people I care about show up late. I just don't get that any more. The goal posts can move. The goal posts do move. It's fine.

I used to get so mad if I bought something online and it was defective in some way. I'd go ape shit on the telephone at the poor customer service staff. I've become very sanguine about missing parts etc. I just accept that sometimes the goal posts move.

I've got my own dog now. A six year old Staffy called Torres. Mad as a hatter. The kids adore him. He adores the kids. He was named Torres after Fernando Torres joined Liverpool Football Club. Fernando left to go to Chelsea Football Club. I'm not a big fan of Chelsea, to say the least.

The dog is now called Tessy. The goal posts move!

6. There are no guarantees, only probabilities

The moment came. I'd been dreading it. As I saw it, I was responsible for the life of two people that I loved so much. One of whom I'd never even met. I was so scared. It was time to get my wife to hospital for the birth of our first child.

I was on edge right through the pregnancy. Once the first signs came that she 'might' be going into labour, I took her straight to the hospital. We were sent home. This happened at least three times before the hospital asked me to keep her at home. When it did come...it was obvious it was coming. I shit myself.

I was in such a panic getting to the hospital. The car got leathered all the way to the hospital that night. On arrival, the nurse asked me for the admission pack. I'd forgotten it. I left my wife at the hospital. The car got leathered all the way back. Grabbed the admission papers. More leathering.

When I arrived back, my wife was screaming but there was no sign of a baby ... yet. A trainee nurse was fiddling around 'down below' with some instrument that breaks waters.

In that sort of situation I'm the kind of person who appears to be in full control. I want to know everything that is going on and why. I compensate for my fear with an attempt to understand and control my environment. It can look very convincing but really I was shitting myself.

Once in labour, things took a turn for the worse. The baby was hooked up to a heart monitor and the nurses were becoming obviously concerned that the heart rate was plummeting. One by one, the room started to fill with people trying to remain calm. I knew that something was wrong. I looked at my wife. I remember thinking, fuck, I'm going to lose them both here.

That thought didn't last long. They started to prep my wife and me for the idea of an emergency c-section. I had to get a grip. My wife was exhausted and high on legal labour drugs. I remember thinking, briefly, that nobody was going to give me any definite guarantees about how this was all going to end.

There are no guarantees, only probabilities. It's my final truth of life. That isn't to say that I might not add more truths in the future, mind. At the start I found myself repeatedly saying the same thing about these truths in my head; I know they are true so why don't I bloody well act on them? Mad!

So if I 'know' they are true, what's changed recently? Effort. That is what has changed. I drill every day on my 'laminate'. Going over and over. Like the yogis who repeat mantras every day. I'm reprogramming my internal hard drive.

I've mentioned before that at first it all felt a little clunky. But now I find I'm simply not aware of the influence it's having on how I react to situations. I just feel calmer, happier and less bothered by stuff.

I believe there are no guarantees, only probabilities. What's more, I'm now living my life around this truth.

As soon as I heard that first scream ... she had me. They took me over to the incubator, cleaned her up a little, then asked me to cut the cord. It was like cutting through a tough piece of squid. My senses were overloaded. I wanted to cry but all I could do was hold my daughter and just stare into her eyes.

My wife was in a bit of a bad way, so I got to stare into my daughters eyes, on my own, for over half an hour. The only time I ever felt that way again was the birth of my second daughter. I've never felt such awe, gratitude, peace of mind, happiness and tearful emotion in my entire life.

And just like that, my life changed forever. For the better, ultimately.

Part Two:
Values

A friend is running a marathon for a well-known heart charity next week. I received a link for his 'justgiving' page. It's really sad looking at a page in honour of a beautiful young girl who has died before her time. I wonder how the father is coping. I'm a father. I think about my own daughters. Then I delete the email.

I want to call him. I call him. I hang up. I want to tell him why I won't support his worthwhile cause. Charities have become corrupt businesses, in my eyes. Senior management earning £200K+, largely from the support of school baking days, pensioners and chuggers. People with pennies supporting multi-millionaires, before the needy get a sniff.

I want to tell him the truth. I want him to understand. I'm not brave enough. I've tried before and it never goes well. I plan to lie. I never got the email. I did mean to donate but I forgot. I've no idea.

Honesty. Should we always tell the truth? Is telling the truth a good thing? Is lying bad? Can you backup your answers with proof? I'm not sure. I don't think it's a truth of life, so I put it in the value basket. It's probably worth having it as a value, a belief that telling the truth is good.

Then I take it out of the value basket, and put it in the waste paper bin. Then I take it back out. I'm not sure.

So what else is in my value basket? What do I value in life? It's hard. I've not had to think about it before. Perhaps that's why I've always blown in the wind.

Figuring them out is one thing. Living by them might be quite another. But by focussing on them every single day I'm able to make sure that my life remains centred around them. Yeah, of course I fall off the wagon from time to time. But by having them documented I'm quickly back out of my own way.

The next chapter will be about my values. Giving to international charitable organisations isn't one of them.

My daughter has brought home a sponsor form. It's for 'bake a cake' day for the refugees in Syria. This weekend I'll be baking cakes. The sponsor form is in the bin. Compromise. One day I'll tell my daughter the truth. The purest form of giving is anonymous to anonymous. I hope she understands.

1. (Health) Man. Meet. Steel.

Thump. Thump. Thump. I could hear the pneumatic pump working hard but something was wrong. The chemical it was supposed to be pumping wasn't being delivered to the right part of the treatment works. The pump sounded different. Heavier. Clunky. Menacing.

2-Chloropropionic acid is an extremely powerful alkylating agent. It's also a neurotoxin. It's not something you want to throw all over yourself. The pump had other ideas.

The exit line on the pump hadn't been opened, and that clunky menacing sound was pressure building up on the weakest part. A fucking jubilee clip. Laughable looking back. Almost.

I can remember the clunky sound stopping. Syrupy liquid hitting me in the eyes. Chest. Mouth. The pump resumed its normal operating sound. Instinctively I ran for the safety shower. Eyes closed. Unfortunately there was a 40T vacuum tanker between me and that shower. Man. Meet. Steel.

Welcome to hazardous waste treatment.

I'd wanted to succeed. Something. Anything. I'd been written off most of my life. The 'naughty little bastard'. I'm prone to daydreaming. I just like staring out of the window on a sunny day. Having ideas. Pondering what we are all doing here on this spinning hunk of rock. But, at the time, I was trying my hardest to impress, get on the ladder, be a 'success'. Become somebody. I'd have done pretty much anything to prove I wasn't a failure.

By the time I got to A&E I was out of the game. I was in complete shock and they rushed me into ... I'm not sure. I have no memory. I have a vague memory of being rigged up to life support machines, monitors, and being frantically pumped with morphine. Everybody should try morphine once in their life. It's the bomb.

I awoke later that night wearing a rough pair of cotton netted underpants. I couldn't feel any pain that night. A beautiful tanned nurse wearing a skimpy little overall came in to bathe me. Seriously, I experienced that but I've no idea if it 'actually' happened; I was so high.

The next day I was in agony. Serious, serious, serious burns all over my body. My skin had already started to blister, pus and peel off. Many weeks later I returned to work.

What stuck with me from that episode was how overwhelmingly I believed that my health was the most important thing in the world. I started taking more exercise, eating better. I felt calmer. Then as the weeks went by, the burns began to heal, and the memories started to fade. And just like that I went back to forgetting about the really important things in life. Values.

We are all guilty at times. We forget about what's important and allow life to overwhelm us. I'm no different. Maybe I'm prone to this more than others. I don't know.

I've created my laminated document to remind me of my values. Not the values that society pushes on us. Not Jay-Z's values. The values that I've sat down and given thought to. The values that feel good when I practise them. The values that have a positive impact on the people around me.

I remind myself every day. Multiple times. I recite them when I'm driving. It's very stabilising, for me, to have a set of values written down. Like a compass being placed on a map. Showing me the direction.

Should I go out with the lads, get bladdered, lap dancers, cocaine, bad relationships, molly, late night kebabs, no sleep, lies about where I've been, £200 bottles of champers, 10 shots of Aftershock, fights, arrests? I'm easily led in this respect. I know I'm easily hijacked. Having money actually makes it worse. There are no brakes in my life.

This is my life now. Map – compass – one day at a time – practising what I preach. I've had so many highs and lows. When I stay healthy it is a firm foundation for everything else in my life. I don't do moderation. It's impossible, for me.

Every morning I get up at around 6.15am. Bring my babies in to see Mum and they all snuggle up. We play a little game where I pretend I'm walking down into a cellar, behind the end of the huge sledge bed. The kids giggle. "Again, again!"

the kids scream. One for the road.

I get in my car. Before I go anywhere I meditate on my breath for 15 minutes. It calms my nervous system. It slows down the bubble machine in my head. Thoughts slow. I review my laminate. Then I drive to my gym. Glass of iced water. I read a few chapters of a good book. Then I write for about an hour. Afterwards I do some cardio, yoga or weights. Take a swim. Jacuzzi. Then I review my laminate.

It's a ritual. I know I'm on the right track because it feels better than the late nights. I'm living my life by the values that I've chosen. It feels good.

I never knew that 2-Chloropropionic acid was a neurotoxin until I looked it up to write this chapter. I felt frightened for a split second. Then one of my truths of life kicked in. Hallelujah.

2. (Laughter) I'm a dopamine addict...

Whenever I go to a restaurant it's my party trick to make a chicken out of a serviette. It always gets a laugh if the people at the table have never seen it before. It feels great to laugh together.

I read somewhere that kids laugh 300 times per day. Adults laugh, on average, 5 times per day. Somehow as we get older we allow life to take away our laughs. One day at a time we laugh less until we are like a clown with a miserable face. Maybe it's just me. I only ever talk about my own life. I've no idea how it works for other people.

Once, I got on a train back from London that was way past its safety limit for carrying passengers. There were no seats, so lots of people were standing around the toilet area. On Virgin trains it's all very Star Trek. Glowing green buttons to open, lock and close the doors.

All very confusing.

I'd drunk too much tea before I got on the train. '*Pppsshhtt*' - the curved door of the Starship Enterprise peeled back. Sitting in front of me was a pensioner on the loo. She hadn't ever passed the NVQ in safe toilet entry on the Enterprise.

It didn't take long until I realised that she couldn't get off the loo to lock the toilet door. Fuck! By now people were tutting and rolling their eyes. I had to go inside and lock the door, so that nobody else could come in.

Skipping forward five minutes, for obvious reasons...

I opened the door. Helped the old lady back to her seat. To the disgust of the people standing outside the toilet door.

I went back to the toilet. Locked! Sense of humour failure.

I've told that story to literally hundreds of people. I've dined out on it. Along with the chicken serviette, it's a nice way to break the ice with strangers. It always gets a laugh. Everybody feels better, the wine flows and people start to tell their own funny/embarrassing stories. Their faces light up. They look happier. More relaxed. Sexier.

It transpires that laughing releases dopamine.

Simply put, the brain releases dopamine as part of a reward-based system. Most types of reward increase dopamine in the brain. Dysfunctions of the brain's natural dopamine system can be responsible for Parkinson's Disease, schizophrenia, ADHD, and Restless Leg Syndrome.

Outside the nervous system, dopamine inhibits norepinephrine release and acts as a vasodilator; in the kidneys, it increases sodium excretion and urine output; in the pancreas, it reduces insulin production; in the digestive system, it reduces gastrointestinal motility and protects intestinal mucosa; and in the immune system, it reduces the activity of lymphocytes. With the exception of the blood vessels, dopamine in each of these peripheral systems has a 'paracrine' function.

Pretty impressive stuff for a 'Dope'...

I've spent the last five years suffering with depression. I had no idea. That's scary. I'm good now. I think I'd spot the warning signs next time. One of the warning signs, for me, is that I laugh a lot less. If I stop laughing it's an early warning sign that something is awry.

Laughing is firmly a value for me. Why wouldn't it be with so many positive benefits for my well-being? Plus it makes others feel good, it's free and it makes you look sexier. It's science, people!

Yesterday I went shopping for a present for my wife. I made a point of telling the cashier a joke about marriage. She laughed. Her face lit up. She had looked so miserable whilst I was waiting in the queue. I noticed how pretty her smile was after I'd told her. I wondered if I looked prettier to her when I laughed with her.

It felt good. It lasted about 15 minutes before it started to fade. I went in the next shop looking for my next fix of dopamine. Legal addictions rock!

So today I'm going to make a long list of all the things that make me laugh. I'm going to create an environment that makes it easier for me to laugh.

Go make a chicken from a serviette today. Be sexy!

3. (Love) That ain't love

We arrived at the party. Sat outside ... We watched. Five of us in a car – and a handgun. I was late teens at the time. I loved my mates. I'd have done anything for them. One of them was in trouble and it was going to get sorted. Permanently.

The door was already open. I had no idea whose house this was and no clue about who was inside. I didn't care. We came for one guy. All we needed to know was whether he was in there.

"Roll. There's the fuckin' rat." Before I could consider the consequences of what was about to happen. I got out of the car. Into the house. A few people saw us burst into the house. We didn't have long before we'd have to be out of sight. This kid got pinned to the floor and told in no uncertain terms that this was his final warning. A round was let off for effect. We vanished as quickly as we arrived.

I look back on that incident. It feels crazy. How different could my life have turned out if that night had gone awry? Could I have handled knowing I'd hurt somebody? What was I thinking about? Those questions didn't enter my head at the time.

Mostly, I was thinking about my mates. A warped sense of love? Actually, it wasn't love at all. It was desire. A desire to be liked. To fit in. To be accepted. Troop mentality. To possess.

Desire.

A firm value in my life these days is love. Proper love. True love. So what is love?

I believe that we are creatures born out of love. Our whole species exists purely because of love. No matter how fleeting. It's a subtle feeling we feel inside of us.

It's those moments when you say, "That's a beautiful colour reflecting off the trees" or "What a gorgeous sunset." The moments when you look in your newborn's eyes as you cut the cord. It's impossible to actually put real love into words.

It's just a feeling. We leave ourselves for a brief moment. We radiate out of ourselves.

When I want to possess something or somebody, I often mistake it for love. It's fine. It's natural that I would do that. I'm part ape. But that ain't love; it's desire.

I am that love right now. I've always been that love. I always will be. I jump around looking for it, but it's right here...right now...right under my nose.

I just need to get out of my own way so that love can function through me.

One of my favourite films is 'Meet Joe Black'. There is a great scene where William Parrish explains to his daughter what he believes love is all about:

Love is passion, obsession, someone you can't live without. If you don't start with that, what are you going to end up with? Fall head over heels. I say find someone you can love like crazy and who'll love you the same way back. And how do you find him? Forget your head and listen to your heart. I'm not hearing any heart. Run the risk. If you get hurt, you'll come back. Because the truth is, there is no sense living your life without this. To make the journey and not fall.

The 'him' in this paragraph is life, in my mind. Be obsessed with living it. Fall head over heels with it. Love life like crazy, and life will love you back like mad. I think I can get there by listening to my heart as I go through life. I'm going to run the risk that I get hurt. Why would I do this? Because I see no sense in living my life without it. I try my best and enjoy the journey. I might fall.

If I live a life full of love – to see the pain in life in the same way that I see the sunset – to rejoice over birth and death – I think that will be a life well lived. I will be fully prepared for whatever comes next. Whatever.

The only gun I carry these days is a heart full of love for life. Some days there is less ammo in it than others. Reload. Roll.

4. (Family) Chasing Ladybirds

When I get up each morning, I can hear my youngest daughter singing to herself in her cot. I get to put her into bed with Mum. She pats me on the back like I've done well. I get the constant feeling that they're here to teach me stuff. I'm listening.

Dressing them and getting them ready for school etc is a nightmare at the moment. They scoot round the kitchen while Mum tries to get a limb into a garment hole. I stay out of the way, if possible. Watching from a safe distance. Grinning.

They get home from school and race into my home office. They always have something to tell me. Artwork to proudly present. Tales to tell. I steal cuddles while they aren't paying attention. I pretend to listen to the drama of the day but honestly, I just like the physical contact. The time to squeeze them and tell them I love them. I like to tease them and pull silly faces.

Teatime can be torturous. Food throwing by the toddler. The older girl refusing to eat her greens. We hide it amongst the potato. Now she won't eat potato. Then the crying starts. Would it be rude if I put my iPod on?!

And I have seen them angry, sulking, mischievous, bored, absorbed, determined, affectionate, passionate, cheerful, relaxed, thoughtful and jealous — moods that they clearly communicate without any need for words.

After tea bike rides to the park. Swings. Roundabouts. Slides. Scooters. Exploring. Laughing. Falling over. Crying. Jokes. Chats. Kisses. Tired legs.

Story time is my favourite part of the day. My eldest daughter takes after me for books. Her room looks like a library. She hides behind the chair most nights. I pretend I don't know where she is. She screams when I find her.

The book is already out. She likes to pick. Very particular about bookmarks. 'Kipper the Dog' is the book of choice tonight. I wrap her in a blanket and sit in Grandpa's old rocking chair.

Afterwards, we turn the lights out. She cuddles in. It's amazing. We both look at the glowing planetarium on her ceiling. She asks the most amazing questions. I tell her the truth. I don't know. She tells me Mummy will know. Maybe, darling. Maybe.

We talk for a while. Tucked into bed. I tell her I love her. Always. No matter what. Even in my darkest days, this part of the day felt special. It always made me smile. Some days it was the only smile.

This is the value of family. My troop. I'd lay down my life for them. We all would. I'm not special in this respect. I've never worked so hard at anything in my life.

I know it gets harder as they get older. They will have their own ideas. They wander away from the nest. Others get to play a bigger role in their lives. They will take risks without understanding or considering the consequences. I'll feel the same way I feel now when I see them hurt themselves. I feel their pain. I know it isn't ever going to be any different. I'll try to be there to pick up the pieces.

My life is about putting out the bins. Changing nappies. Providing. Building Lego towers. Cutting grass. It's a long way from how my life used to be. I do it for my family. It's a duty and an honour. I accept it, gladly. There was some resistance, initially.

Tonight Kipper will chase a ladybird around the garden. And I will steal a hundred cuddles.

5. (Assertiveness) Sea Bass

We sat in a country club. Lunch was served. I'd picked the sea bass. I've no idea why I picked sea bass. I had no idea what it was going to taste like. I'd grown up on free school meals. I thought this is what you ordered after you had escaped a concrete jungle.

See also: Castle Lafite Rothschild Pauillac 1996

The guy sitting in front of me was a nervous wreck. There is so much that you don't learn when you grow up on the streets. For a long time I had no idea how to order at a restaurant. No idea how to put up a shelf or do an oil change. Still haven't. However, you learn how to read people. Spidey senses. This guy was a walking time bomb, mentally.

Over lunch he asked me to run his entire business. More to the point, he wanted it restructuring. He was a man of considerable means. But ... no backbone.

I had no idea how I'd go about it. He knew I didn't have a clue. But he had been told that I had one unusual quality. An apparent ease with dispensing with people who didn't cut the mustard. I called it 'pulling off chickens' heads'. Quick. An element of surprise. Make it painless. Sudden.

Maybe. What nobody knew is that I'd sit up all night for days before going over and over it in my head. Afterwards I'd endure the lowest lows a human could suffer. Inflicting planned suffering onto another human being is the worst feeling in the world. Unless you're a psychopath and your head doesn't have the right genetic material to feel remorse.

The only way I knew how to handle this whirlwind of emotions was to be assertive. Make up my mind and act. Spell out what was going to happen and leave no room for anybody to offer alternatives. Assertion.

When my first-born took her first breath I was given the dubious privilege of cutting the cord. Actually, it was an incredible experience. Recommended. Afterwards, I sat there looking into her eyes. Humans lack the nuanced language to put into words the experience of looking into your own child's eyes. For me, it was like looking into my own soul.

I took a decision right there to change direction. To get off the bus going in the wrong direction. I had no idea which bus I would get on next. But I did know I was on the wrong bus; going in the wrong direction. So I got off.

I spent the next five years sitting at that bus stop. Lost. Wondering what bus I should get on next. Sometimes people would come along and chat whilst I sat at that stop. Offering advice. Sometimes I'd think about hopping on another bus and then quickly change my mind. It was so tempting to get back on the original bus and continue the journey I thought I was destined to take.

Depressed wasn't the word.

I read an awful lot of Buddhist texts whilst I was sitting at that metaphorical bus stop. I thought it had some good answers. I still do. The problem was that whilst I was on retreats it felt awesome. Such peace of mind, and a feeling of deep love for everybody and everything. The problems started when I plonked myself back into the real world. A world of business, family, strangers, capitalism, and anger. It didn't square for me.

I'd put Buddha's words into practice. Sometimes it felt good, but often part of me felt abused. Some people, sometimes, would take the piss. It rattled me. Couldn't people see how hard I was trying to turn my life around?

Who was I?! I thought I knew. Now I was questioning everything. I'd look around me and think...OK, he looks like he's got things sussed. So I'd copy. Try and play the nice guy. Didn't work for me. It was important that I worked out who I was, and what I stood for. What did I believe? What did I value? What did I think life was all about?

I wrote it all down. Specifically for me. Fuck Moses and his tablets. Never trust a man with a beard.

I realised there is a part of me that will never lie down. I need to protect that part. Otherwise, I get very very unsettled. Understanding that we are unique is one of the biggest lessons I've ever learnt.

Assertive. The ability to be self-assured and confident without being aggressive. It's a core value for me.

I've had to learn that it's not life or death. I'd often come across as aggressive. That isn't how I want to come across. It's a skill I'm learning to get better at. I want to give freely without worrying that people are going to take advantage of my loved ones or me. Deciding how best to navigate those waters used to feel like a proper headache. Now, I think I've got it licked.

The sea bass came. The biggest plate I'd ever seen. Beautifully garnished. It was fucking bland. I never ordered sea bass again.

6. (Happiness) A date with Ziggy...

I sat in my kitchen. It was bigger than the previous downstairs of my old house. It was Xmas Eve. I'd not shaved for days. My kid rode a plastic zebra, 'Ziggy', round and round. I was numb.

Everything I'd ever wanted...I had. Lovely wife. wonderful kids. Big house. No mortgage. Plenty of dosh. Nice cars. Holidays whenever we wanted. Good long-standing business. Nice friends. Every goal I'd ever set I'd smashed! Now what?!

I sat there. Numb. I muttered something stupid to my wife. I don't remember what she said back. She had worked out that I was depressed and unhappy. She also knew it had nothing to do with her. We've chatted about it recently and it amazes me how grounded she is.

Earlier in the year I'd run off to New Zealand. I'd convinced myself that I was looking for a place to emigrate. In hindsight I just think I was like an escaped psych ward patient who had gone over the wall. Every day I'd drive to some new place, find digs, eat and then go to bed. I think I was possibly insane at this point in my life. Joking aside, I wasn't in a great space, mentally. I was looking for something. I just didn't know what I was looking for.

Six weeks later, I skyped the wife. She told me I looked awful and I should come home. I went home. Nothing changed.

By now I had no energy whatsoever. I tried to exercise and it would take me days in bed to recover. I wanted to eat and sleep, nothing else – except an addiction to sex. Great mix. Horny. Chronic fatigue. On the days I had more energy I'd go over and over things in my head. Trying to work it all out.

Why wasn't I happy? What is happiness anyway?

In January 2014 I'd just about given up. Lost cause. A pilot in charge of a plane that was in a terminal dive. I was getting irrationally angry at everyone and anything. I'm not somebody to be around when I get in that frame of mind.

I was walking through Waterstones one day. Spotted 'Chimp Paradox' sitting on the shelf. "Usual self help bollocks," I said to myself. I went home and for some reason decided to take another look on Amazon. Up popped Ronnie O'Sullivan's book review. I like Ronnie. I've always felt I was wired the same way even though I've never spoken to him. The review was amazing. I bought the book because Ronnie's review convinced me to give it a go.

The whole plot of the book I'm writing is about my experiences leading up to buying that book. How my life changed for the better after reading it. How I implemented the exercises into my life. Ultimately it's about how I became happy. Possibly for the first time in my life. My suffering humbled me. It made me a better person, ultimately.

Happiness is a choice, albeit it has been a difficult one for me at times. It's something that I have to work on every day. It's one of my values. Along with love, laugh, family etc. I think being happy is different for every single one of us. I had to work out what it meant to me.

For me, I work hard to maintain a base level of contentment. I remove as much stress, anxiety and concern as possible. I eat right, meditate, keep good company, exercise and remind myself how fortunate I am. I take care to look after my close circle and I'm cautious about who I allow in it. The biggest thing I've changed is to rehearse my 'laminate'. Every single day I'm going over and over it in my head, three or four times a day. It's had an amazing effect on my baseline level of contentment.

I've found it really useful to make a mental note each night of what the next day's main theme will be. Writing, coding, snowboarding, swimming with my girls, meeting a friend etc. Every day has a central theme. Purpose.

I'm never going to be the type of person that walks round beaming ear to ear. I still have my moments but I'm learning to spot them and I've got a drill for addressing them.

I've learnt that by adding stuff into my life I can elevate levels of happiness. I took up snowboarding recently. It's created novelty, fun and a potential new social circle for me. I'm committed to writing every day as it feels great to be creative, and I get a sense of achievement from finishing each piece.

Part of me is never satisfied with anything I achieve or possess. I was never the type of person to celebrate my successes. Onto the next one. I'm more aware than ever of this loop running inside my head and I work actively to combat it. It's important to my sense of happiness that I pat myself on the back for the smallest of wins.

For all the money I've made, I still think I'm going to the poor house. I've started going out of my way to prove to myself that it's not going to happen. I'm tight fisted by nature. I'd rather shop at Greggs for dinner than go to a restaurant. I've got clothes I wear all the time that are over ten years old. It's a very outdated loop running inside my internal computer. Scarcity. I'm working on it. I'm starting to really enjoy the things that I do have. They might not last forever.

Relationships are important. Luckily, I'm with the right person. My wife is my hero. She is amazing. I wouldn't want to be with anybody else. She knows it. She helps me develop as a person. She brings out the best in me. She puts me first. She accepts me as I am. Warts and all. She is also as fit as a butcher's dog.

I went through a phase during my dark period where I no longer knew who I was. I've had to sit down and work it out from scratch. I know exactly who I am now. I underestimated what a powerful concept that is. It's made a huge difference to my self-esteem.

I've stopped trying to impress people so much. I accept my

shortcomings. All that I can do is my best. I'm trying to live my life, by my values, every single day. Laugh; love; family; assertive; happiness; health; creativity and friendship. This is what I expect of myself. Something for others to measure me by. These things add to my life. They create the conditions for happiness.

One thing that has helped me enormously is to have a mental list of things that improve my immediate mood. Sometimes I still get waves of 'shittyness'. They come without warning. I catch myself and force a happy activity onto myself. PS3, tidying up in the garden, call a friend, run, yoga, walk the dog or meditate. Really good mood enhancers.

Planning future events also helps. We sit down and book holidays way into the future nowadays. Setting outrageous goals also helps. Pie in the sky ideas. All of these things elevate my happiness beyond baseline contentment.

I could write a whole book on this subject; maybe I will.

My kids have nearly grown too big for Ziggy. I'm going to keep him. I never want to forget how low you can get if you 'allow' it to happen.

7. (Creativity). Get rich quick schemes...

I sent off for a get rich quick scheme. I'd read all about it in the Mersey Mart, a free rag they kept at the back of the library. It promised you could be rich beyond your wildest dreams. I could escape this shit hole I'd been born into.

Maybe it would contain all the answers I'd been looking for. How to pick yourself up off the floor when you're out of luck and on your 'uppers'.

What did dawn on me was that spending money to buy other people's ideas is nuts. Mad. So I stopped it. Thankfully I was very young. Lots of time to have my own ideas. I'd write down pages and pages of ideas. I carried a notebook everywhere with me.

Recipes. Business. Articles. Inventions. Friends. Travel. Ideas for everything. Mostly how to get rich.

One time, I wrote to Richard Branson. I offered him some of my ideas and asked him if he'd like to come to my mum's for a pan of scouse. I got a nice letter back; signed personally. It meant the world to me. Branson had a massive impact on me. Here was a guy who had mad ideas and then just made it all happen.

I've still got that letter all these years later. It taught me that if you have an idea and follow through ... that magic could happen. Anybody could have written that letter. I did. The cost was a stamp and the risk of looking stupid.

I reckon we all have the capacity for creativity. It's like a muscle. It needs to be exercised. Constantly. If you get an arm trapped under a rock in the world's deepest ravine, in the middle of nowhere, you need to be prepared. It's the idea muscle that will get you out of the stickiest situations.

In 2008 people were literally shitting themselves about their jobs, homes, family and lifestyles. We live in a £1.3Tr economy. How much money do you want? It's out there waiting to be sucked up by people with strong idea muscles. Most of the world's dominant companies today were started during the Great Depression.

Ideas are one thing. Execution is another. Or to put it another way, having ideas is simply thinking about creativity. Like masturbation for the mind. But execution is creativity. The real deal. It's the creators that this world rewards.

I have lots of ideas. Many of them never get past first base. I started a comic recently called "Facepleb'. People laughed. That's OK. People laughed when I started my first business. People laughed when I started blogging. People laughed when I said I was doing triathlons. People laughed when I said I was writing a book to publish. People have been laughing at me my whole life.

It's fine. I get it. No hard feelings. It's the price of success. Being laughed at.

Creativity is something I value. It helped get me out of the concrete jungle. At times it's saved my life. Literally. It's helped me picture what the future could hold. It helps me push past sticking points. It helps me ignore the laughter.

The parcel arrived. 'Get rich quick'. I opened it, hoping to find an answer. Predictably, I didn't. Sad face.

8. (Friendship) The phone doesn't ring at weekends

The phone rang constantly. Hauliers wanting to know where a site contact was. Staff wanting to know how to reboot the servers. Customers wanting to know where a haulier was. Solicitors wanting to know when they were getting paid. It never stopped.

Except at the weekend. The phone would lie silent in my pocket, like a small curled up animal that had gone to sleep.

I can't recall when I first noticed that it didn't ring at weekends. I was just glad of the respite. But once I'd noticed, the silence was deafening.

I started to notice that my wife would get friends calling. Family calling. Siblings texting. I got ...silence. Sometimes it would ring and I'd hear the mechanical tones of an automated sales call.

You get what you focus on in life. I'd focused on business for so long that I'd forgotten how to be a good friend. So why would anybody call?!

The whole point about writing down my values, thinking about my values, is that I want my life to be centred around them. I want them to execute in my brain so fast that I'm no longer conscious of them. If you asked a member of the SAS what they were thinking about as they entered the hijacked plane and shot four terrorists, they'd tell you that they don't think anything. It's automatic. Drilled. Slick.

To achieve this I practise every single day. I rehearse what my values are. Over and over. Every single day. I'm writing this book to share how these values have had a deep impact on my life. Not to create a New York best sellers, but so that it seeps deep into my internal hard drive.

I've got two main thoughts on friendship, the last of my values. The first is that some of the friends I've had aren't so good for me. They have values that aren't aligned with how I actually want to live my life. I'm easily encouraged into activities that are destructive to me and people around me that I love. Part of me is very easily encouraged. Chimp!

Making sure that I take stock of who is in my gang is essential.

Back in the day I was very protective of who I allowed in my gang, but for all the wrong reasons. It'd be all about who was good with women, did they take recreational drugs, could they handle their ale, could they fight, were they popular?

Nowadays I want my gang to value love, compassion, society, respect of others, creativity, health, support, adventure, exploration. It sounds harsh but if their values aren't more or less aligned with mine then I don't want to be around them. As I said, part of me is easily led in some ways. Although in other ways I'm as stubborn as a mule.

The second thought about friendship is that I want to focus on my gang almost to the exclusion of everybody else. I don't intend going around being rude to people, but I do intend keeping it light. I don't want to confide in people outside of my gang.

I believe it's a mistake for me to try and befriend every single person on the planet without considering what their value system is. You could be the nicest person in the world but if you want to go out and get smashed every weekend then we ain't going to get off first base.

When you get on a plane they tell you in the event of an emergency put on your own oxygen mask before tending to those around you. This is how I view friendship. In order for me to be a good friend, I have to get myself in a good place first. By keeping a close circle of friends who share similar values, I'm able to put my own oxygen mask on first.

One of the surprising benefits of thinking/writing about my values is that it dawned on me pretty quickly that I was actually describing to myself who I was. Have you ever asked yourself: Who are you? Could you do an elevator pitch to somebody?

Earlier this year I had no idea who I was any more!

Here's who I am.

I believe that as much as I'd like life to be fair....it isn't. I deal with it. I believe that nothing lasts forever. I believe that I might not wake up tomorrow. I believe that not everybody will like me. It sucks. I believe that the goal posts move. I believe that there are no guarantees.

I value health, love, laughter, family, assertiveness (my chimp begged me to put that in), happiness, creativity and friendship.

I think life is about doing your best and enjoying the journey. I think you can only control your efforts and not the fruits of your labour. I think I should always give freely what people need, but flip a coin on giving what they want. I want to look for the good in others.

All of this is a work in progress. I'm getting better every day at getting out of my own way and being the person I actually am. I'm lowering the incidence of hijack. This is what I'm working towards.

I drill every day just in case I'm asked to enter a hijacked plane. Frag grenade, sonars down, smoke grenade tossed. Blap-blap-blap. Mission accomplished. Hostiles down.

Part Three:
What is life all about?

1. Give people what they need. Flip a coin on giving them what they want

It's October 2013. Five long and draining years since I'd watched my daughter being born, cut the cord and realised I was on a bus going in the wrong direction. I'd sat at that metaphorical bus stop for so long. Just trying to figure out what I was supposed to do next. I felt so lost and lonely.

I'd spent the majority of that time studying Buddhism. At its essence is the concept of emptiness. Conceptually beautiful; practically useless. At first, I struggled with developing minds of compassion and love. I felt major resistance. Then, as the Buddhists would say, my heart just opened up.

I started looking around to find people who were struggling that I could help. I honestly thought this was what I should be doing. At first it was old folk crossing the road. People in shops who couldn't reach the top shelves. That kind of stuff. Easy helping.

Then I'd give everybody I met a big smile. Like they were all my friends. One big cosmic family. This provoked some strong responses in others. Good and bad.

I'd give people money. People I hadn't seen for years. People I hardly knew. Strangers. Homeless. One time I gave some guy £100 in the street. I'd watched him begging in the rain while I waited for my wife to come out of a shop. He thanked me and told me he couldn't wait to get bladdered later that night.

I'd offer to support/help people in business. They wanted my contacts. They didn't want my advice. I suppose I wanted some company. Maybe I just wanted to be liked. One guy shouted at me when I said that I didn't want to buy his services.

It's really odd. In 2008 nobody fucked with me. Nobody. It would have been unheard of for somebody to shout at me. No matter who they were. I had a demeanour that stopped people dead in their tracks. I didn't put up with people's bullshit, and they could tell as soon as I walked into a room. The problem was, as has often been the case, I took it all too far.

Fast forward to 2013.....I'd lent an old 'friend' a few grand. I genuinely wanted nothing back. I was happy to help him out of a hole. It was supposed to be to help him get a business off the ground. Next thing I knew he was on holiday. Some start to a new business.

When he got back it wasn't long before he was asking me for a few more grand. I asked him to send me a business plan and a cash flow forecast.

To help him get going I suggested that he do some work on my house. I spelt out that it was to be normal rates. Not mates' rates. I wanted an invoice, and it was to be totally professional. I didn't want him doing it for free. He turned up on the first day three hours late, and only stayed an hour. My missus wasn't impressed, to say the least.

Supposedly he was coming back the next day. I waited in all day. No show. No phone call. This was now a recurring theme in my life. I was attracting dickheads who took the piss.

At this point I genuinely thought about getting back on the bus I'd gotten off. Why bother being nice to people if it just encouraged them to abuse my new-found goodwill? I struggled with this more than probably anything else.

The answer came out of the blue. I was listening to Russell Simmons give a talk about the homeless in the US. Russell is a mentor to me. Informally. I can relate a lot to his message. I'm no billionaire, but I did come from quite a tough background and manage to make a fist of my life.

It wasn't so much what Russell said; it was more his attitude towards people in general. He talked about how *some* homeless people actually have everything they need. Good health. Lots of recreational time. Roof over the head, of sorts. Yet they spend most of their day with a hand out. Seemingly unwilling to serve others. I thought back to the homeless guy I'd given some money to. I remembered my old mate not turning up to work, but always wanting more money. I recalled the guy who wanted me to pay him for services I didn't need or want.

A common theme emerged. Lots of these people rocking up in my life wanted things they never needed. My mate needed some encouragement and a reality check; not more money. The homeless guy needed a leaflet for Alcoholics Anonymous; not £100 for vodka. The business guy needed hanging up on rather than trying to calm him down.

"Give people what they need freely, but flip a coin on giving them what they want."

My kids want ice cream all the time. They love it. I like seeing their happy faces as they smear it all around their gorgeous little gobs. But too much isn't good for them. They just don't see it. They might want it, but they don't need it. However, they always need a cuddle. No matter what. I never stop cuddling them and telling them how much I love them. Particularly after I've told them off.

I treat everybody this way now. It really was the missing piece in my own personal jigsaw. People don't take the piss any more. But neither do they dread having to deal with me. It's a much more balanced approach. It was the first bus stop I arrived at when I got on the bus going in the right direction.

Some people need a kind word. Some people need a little money. Some people need a kick in the arse. And some people need nothing. Most people want, want, want......flip a coin.

2. You can only do your best. Enjoy the journey

Steve Fugate decided to trek across the entire breadth of the United States of America. He could have had no idea what would happen next as he set off across the country.

Halfway across he received news that his eldest son had put a gun in his mouth and pulled the trigger. Devastating news for any parent. Steve returned home to deal with matters.

After burying his son, he decided to finish the trek he had started in honour of his late son. Towards the end of that journey he received even more bad news. His daughter had been found dead.

How does a parent cope after losing both their kids?! I've no idea. Truly. We expect that life has a natural order. We expect our children to outlive us.

After burying his daughter, Steve set out to finish the trek. Only this time it was a mission. A mission to impress on people across the country that life is to be loved. No matter how big your problems seem, life is to be loved. Here is a link to an interview that Steve gave for a documentary about his life. I can't do justice to what Steve tries to accomplish every day so

I'll let him speak for himself. Watch the link; you will not regret it. http://youtu.be/inMiPIuNXsU

If I was able to pass on some wisdom to my great great grandchildren it would be that you can only ever do your best in life. So enjoy the journey. I've a picture of Steve that I look at every single day to remind me. Doing your best and enjoying the journey is one of the things that I think life is all about.

I remind myself of this at least five times per day. Over and over, silently, in my head. It's a lovely mantra. So reassuring. Because you can only ever try your best in life. We sometimes kid ourselves into thinking somehow we are magically going to be successful at everything we try our hands at. It was never true for me. I only ever talk for myself. Maybe you are different. I can't know.

I'm giving a public speech this week. I've never done one before. I've had the opportunity to do so on many occasions but I always offered excuses for why I couldn't do it. Holiday, illness, bad timing etc. The truth was that I thought people wouldn't be interested in what I had to say. I thought they'd talk about me behind my back. I thought. I thought. I thought.

This week is different. I'm going to talk about how I managed to get my demons under control to improve my life. There may be somebody in the audience who has always felt the same way but hasn't found any answers. Maybe how I've managed to turn my life around will offer some clues for them. Maybe not. Who knows?!

I've an honest intention to share some information that has really benefited me. I've got the basic tools: voice, legs, brain. I've prepared what I'm going to talk about. I'm sure I will feel a little nervous beforehand. I also treated myself to some new 'Samba' and a new pair of 'Ted's'. On the day I'm going to get my pap shaved; nice and fresh. But I'm going to try and do my best. And I'm going to enjoy the experience.

So many times in the past I've sabotaged myself. Opportunities missed because I couldn't keep my emotions in check. Does everybody feel this way? Sometimes I wonder if it's just me. That's in the past now. I've developed a method for dealing with it. I don't mind talking about my past experiences if it helps others, but I'm genuinely not focused on the past any more.

The future looks exciting.

3. You can only control your efforts alone and not the fruits of your labour

I sat in a cold, damp, office on the dockside at Birkenhead. Alone. It was the middle of winter and it'd been raining hard for days. The sky was dark grey. I'd been coming here for nearly six months. Staring at the phone on my desk. Tapping away at a spreadsheet. I noticed that if I increased the top line sales figure the bottom line profit went up. My first business.

Only on this day it was my day of reckoning. The day I'd sink or swim. Cash flow is like oxygen to a business. Why was I so scared of making cold calls? Just a transfer of sound waves down a copper cable. It felt like life or death. I wanted them to call me. Tell them how bloody good I was, and how much I knew about hazardous waste regulations. Nobody cared.

Eminem was on the radio.

"Look, if you had one shot, or one opportunity

To seize everything you ever wanted, one moment

Would you capture it or just let it slip? Yo!"

Those lyrics were responsible for what happened next. I'd daydreamed about being a successful businessman my entire life. If I didn't do this now then the dream was over. I thought I'd never get a second chance.

After clearing my throat I lifted the phone. Dialled from a pre-prepared list, and spoke into the receiver. My voice trembled.

"His palms are sweaty, knees weak, arms are heavy

There's vomit on his sweater already, mom's spaghetti."

The receptionist put me through to the potential customer. I panicked. Hung up.

But I'd survived. I went for a walk.

The rest is history. I can make 60-70 calls an hour when I put my mind to it. I've never met anybody that can do telesales the way I do it. When I lift the telephone I never expect to make a sale. I never try and talk anybody into anything. I focus on lifting the receiver. Over and over.

My answer, the only answer that works for me, is to remember Krishna's axiom from the *Bhagavad Gita*. It goes something like this.

"You can only control your efforts, but not the fruits of your labour."

I recognise that what people make of my efforts is only loosely related to its quality. I've seen shit succeed. Sometimes shit beats the hell out of great stuff. Some of the poorest quality work I've ever done got the biggest pay days. Equally, some of the stuff I see as my best work just didn't chime for people.

Success. Failure. Two sides of the same coin. Both illusions. You do your best and the universe takes care of the rest. How you feel about the work and its reception matters.

In the end, for me, what matters is what you think about your work. No other opinion counts. I try to do work these days that I can be proud of. I share what I love.

This is life. This is what I believe.

4. Look for the good in others

In my younger years I used to work on the scaffold. Tough job. Shit pay. I'd only agreed to do it because I wanted to tour America and needed the dough. A mate of mine, Jay, had a brother working as a handyman at a 'Camp America' in the Catskill Mountains. Former training home of the legendary boxer Mike Tyson.

Fast forward. We arrived at JFK with a bag each and a couple of grand between us. His brother was supposed to meet us at the airport. It was about 3am. JFK is a freaky place at that time of morning. Shady looking Mexicans had already started to weigh us up. Thankfully, I was quite handy and Jay was a six foot two ex-squaddie who had literally just got out of a two stretch in the 'Glasshouse'.

Just as we had decided to give his brother up for dead he showed up. Some yarn about the car breaking down on the highway and having to take it to be mended. It turned out to be one of the few true yarns that this lad ever told me. So off we went back to the garage ... in the Bronx.

Arriving at 3am in the Bronx is another story for another time. Funny. Very funny, looking back. Scary at the time.

The upshot was that the car couldn't be fixed. We had to get a taxi from the Bronx to Catskill. $150 later we arrived at this little shack in the middle of the woods. This wasn't the private beach house that we'd been promised. Fuck it, I'd have the conversation tomorrow. So we broke open a few bottles.

It turned out that we had landed next to a lake. The private beach with cloned 'Pammies' running about was the other side of the lake, and it was full of 7-10 year olds playing volleyball. Jimmy Savile might have been happy......but I wasn't.

There was no point in pulling this lad over the coals. He was good fun, I liked him and we had to make the most of it. Besides, we didn't have the money for more than a week's worth of food and digs, never mind a return flight home. It wasn't long before the landlady arrived asking for the rent. Er.

This wasn't the first time I'd been in a pickle. I've always favoured honesty over bullshitting people. Not because I'm intrinsically honest. I just can't handle the stress of keeping up lies over a prolonged period. I'd rather tell people exactly what is going on so that I know where I stand. So I went off to find the landlady.

Miriam. That was her name. I've never forgotten her. She was an 80-year-old Jewish lady who stayed in Catskill in the summer to escape the heat of Florida. She was clearly no push over. I knew that the first time I looked into her eyes. I'd seen those eyes before...in the mirror. I told her the truth. She asked me how much money I had. I showed her. She took it. We stayed. Negotiations over.

Problem was that we now had no money for food etc. Or at least, little. I'd not quite shown Miriam all of the money we had. You can take the lad out of Bootle but you can never take Bootle out of the lad.

Anyhow. We had enough money to feed us for about a week. We'd worry about what to do next once it ran it. We went to the only local pub for 50 miles that night. Got rat arsed, ate pizza and spent the lot. The motivation to think ahead was lost on the three of us. It was a good night though.

We got up the next day. Banging hangover. "What's for brekkie?" asked Jay. Oh yeah, we've got no money, I thought. "Fuck all, lad," I replied.

Next door was a gang of hillbillies that Miriam had warned me away from. "White trash," she had called them. They were a bunch of rednecks who drank 'hooch', played loud music and seemed to have an endless supply of kids running about.

I knocked on the door. The leader, Richie, opened the door. Spat. Closed it. So I sat down on his porch. It was scorching and I just wanted a bit of shade for two minutes.

The door opened. It was left open. Richie sat down in front of the telly and didn't utter another word. His wife invited me in. We had bacon and eggs, beer and a toke on a spliff. That is how my relationship with Richie began.

Miriam called round that night. She had seen me at Richie's. She seemed genuinely concerned for my welfare. I told her he was a bit quirky but he'd given me some breakfast. "White trash," she repeated. It was my first taste of how racially divided America was... but not the last. Richie was no better. He would often call Miriam the 'fuckin' Yid'. This was all alien to me. I had Italian mates, African mates, Greek mates, Jewish mates. I grew up in Liverpool, which is a major port. It was a melting pot.

And yet, for all the bad behaviour, racism and scarcity mentality, these people were feeding me. Sharing their home with me. They took me into their families. They made me laugh. They took me places. They invited me to family gatherings to meet their grand kids. They found odd jobs for me to do – that probably didn't need doing – and they paid me for it. They would sit for hours and tell me about their own lives.

If I'd listened to my mates I'd have never gone round to Miriam's house and told her how it was. I'd have labelled her. Ignored her. Likely gotten her back up.

If I'd listened to Miriam I'd have never gone round to Richie's. I'd have scowled at him with deep suspicion whenever I crossed his path. It'd probably have ended in violence one drunken night.

For most of my life I've always preferred to look for the good in others. I think that is an unusual trait for where I grew up. Sometimes I'd get burnt thinking that way, but it just felt better. People, more often than not, surprised me.

That changed, big time, when I started getting involved in the world of business. I'd been around gangsters growing up but they had nothing on some of the people I met during my early years of business. So I started to defend myself and lost the ability to see the good in others.

That was a mistake. I'm now correcting it. Back to school.

It's easy to find the bad in people. It's too bloody easy. It's more difficult to find the good – which is presumably why so few people bother trying. Funny thing is that when you do point their good traits out to them, they often start improving their behaviour towards you. And besides, it feels better.

When I returned to the UK I was glad to be home. I sent handwritten letters to Miriam for years. She wrote back. Then they stopped. RIP Miriam. Your 'Kosher' chicken pie was divine.

What's Next?

I cut my hedge yesterday. It's a beast. It took me nearly four hours. I'd bought a petrol mower. Put it together myself. The sun was blistering. My kids were planting runner beans in the garden with Mum. I watched them as I cut the hedge.

People walked past as I cut the outer side of the hedge. I smiled at every single one of them. Some put their heads down. That's OK; I used to feel that way. A few cracked a joke. One lady, Ingrid, stopped for a chat. I genuinely enjoyed it.

At the beginning of this year I'd never have cut my own hedge. I'd always paid somebody else to do it. I was scared that I'd do it wrong. Scared that the neighbours would complain about my ladder blocking the path. Scared that I'd cut my arm off. But mainly scared that somebody would criticise the end result. Like it was life or death. Like it was tied to my own self worth.

The hedge episode is true. But it's also a metaphor for my entire life really. Cutting that hedge was a big deal for me. It was a fresh start. I'm no longer scared to live. I've stopped getting in my own way.

My wish is that when my daughters read this book they understand their dad better. I love you both, unconditionally. I tell you all the time but it never does any harm to see it written down.

Live your life. Love it. Realise that you will have times when you're filled with fear but that you can overcome these feelings. Think about what you value and try to create a life around these values. Don't allow other people to dictate your values. Think for yourself.

Ultimately, people always want to know what you did with your life. If anybody asks me, I'll tell them I spent it with my girls. I wrote this book for you both.

Oh, and as I'm so pedantic I've left you a reading list at the back. As you undoubtedly know, Daddy is a book worm.

Appendix 1: Reading List

Chimp Paradox by Dr Steve Peters

Happy Yoga by Steve Ross

Do You! by Russell Simmons

Super Rich by Russell Simmons

Anti Fragile by Nasim Taleb

Life of Pi by Yann Martel

The Personal MBA by Josh Kaufman

Modern Buddhism by Geshe la Kelsang

The Power of Now by Eckhart Tolle

Making the Modern World by Vaclav Smil

The China Study by T. Colin Campbell

Why We Get Fat by Gary Taubes

You Are Here by Thich Nhat Hanh

So Good They Can't Ignore You by Cal Newport

Street Smart by Jim Rogers

Mastery by Robert Green

Fear by Fifty Cent and Robert Green

The War of Art by Steven Pressfield

Bounce by Matthew Syed

Search Inside Yourself by Chade-Meng Tan

Appendix 2: Laminate

Truths

Values

Life Force

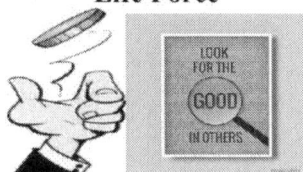

About the Author

Originally a professional chemist in the hazardous waste sector, Paul Doran created Axion Waste Solutions (AWS). AWS became one of the leading hazardous waste brokers in the UK. Paul went on to have success with a number of start up companies. Business success allowed Paul to return to university in 2008 to study Computer Forensics, and he recently graduated with a first class honours degree. In 2012 Paul went travelling and blogging around New Zealand. During this time away from his family Paul began to ask himself some soul searching questions, which ultimately led to a period of writing and reflection.

Paul lives on the Wirral with two beautiful daughters and his wife – not forgetting his adorable but slightly nutty Staffordshire Bull Terrier, Tessy. Paul now spends most his time reading, writing and trading the stock markets.

Printed in Great Britain
by Amazon